Animc

Contents

written by John Lockyer

1

Most places have special emergency services.
Police, fire, and ambulance are the emergency
services that help to keep people safe.
Animal rescue is an emergency service that
helps to keep animals safe.

Animal rescue workers save wild animals, farm animals, and pets that are homeless, hurt, or lost. They look after many different animals, such as birds, rabbits, dogs, goats, cows, donkeys, and horses.

3

vet

Vets and nurses are animal rescue workers. They are trained to know what is wrong with sick or injured animals. When vets have to operate on an animal, they wear special clothes. Their clothes must be clean to stop germs spreading to the animal.

4

In some places, there are rangers who look after wild animals. They work in forests and parks to check that the animals keep safe and healthy. Rangers also make sure that people are safe from wild animals.

ranger

animal rescue center

If an animal is homeless or sick or injured, it can be taken to an animal rescue center. Most small animals are transported in cages because they get frightened and may run away. In an emergency, an animal can be transported to the rescue center in an animal rescue ambulance.

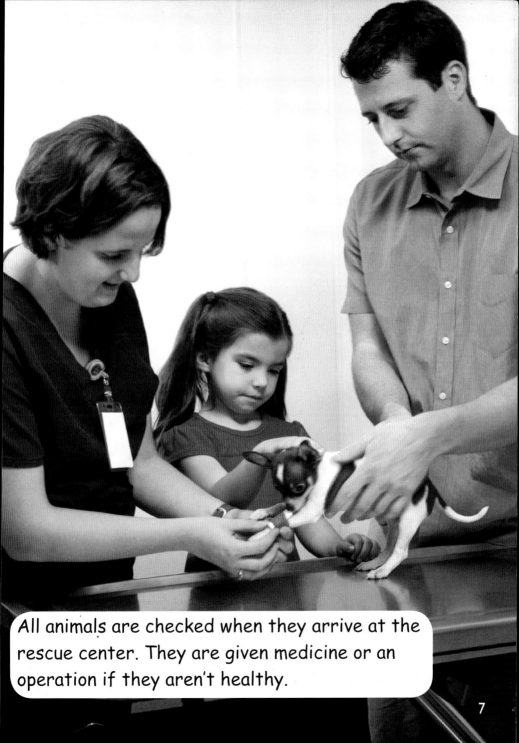

All animals are checked when they arrive at the rescue center. They are given medicine or an operation if they aren't healthy.

A large animal rescue center has buildings with many rooms. There are different rooms for cats, kittens, dogs, and birds. They also have fields for horses and farm animals. These rescue centers often have a hospital where vets take care of sick animals.

volunteer

Volunteers do a lot of the work at rescue centers. They learn from vets and rangers how to care for animals. They feed the animals with healthy food. Volunteers clean animals with brushes, scissors, combs, and shampoo. They even brush some animals' teeth!

Need a
Good
Home!

Volunteers clean cages. There are small cages for small animals. Large animals have bigger cages so that they can move around. Straw, newspaper, and soft bedding must be changed every day.

Some animals, such as dogs, need lots of exercise, so the volunteers take them for walks every day.

10

Many animals at rescue centers are frightened because they have been lost or hurt. Vets, rangers, nurses, and volunteers give extra time and care to these animals.

Animal rescue centers are not homes for animals. As soon as the animals are healthy, rescue workers try to find them a good home. They teach new pet owners how to care for their animals properly.

Sometimes sick or injured wild animals are taken to rescue centers. These animals need special care, so wild-animal vets from zoos often check and care for them. When wild animals are strong and healthy again, they are set free in their own habitat.

whale stranding

Large wild animals that are in trouble, such as whales and dolphins, cannot be taken to a rescue center. When whales get stranded on a beach, volunteer rescue workers come quickly to help them.

The rescue workers keep the whales wet and try to keep them afloat. They even put sunblock on them! They have to wait for the tide to come in. The volunteers stay with the whales until they can swim back out to sea.

Animal rescue workers love to work with eagles, rabbits, seagulls, and donkeys. They just love to help any animals!